Original title:

Crystalline Frost

Author: Johan Kirsipuu

ISBN HARDBACK: 978-9916-79-876-8

ISBN PAPERBACK: 978-9916-79-877-5

ISBN EBOOK: 978-9916-79-878-2

Embrace of the Chill at First Light

The dawn whispers softly in the sky,
Frost kisses the leaves, a gentle sigh.
Morning dew glistens on blades of grass,
A world awakes, as the shadows pass.

Birds flutter timidly from nest to tree,
Their songs weave through the air, wild and free.
The sun peeks out, a golden embrace,
Warming the chill in this tranquil place.

A Dance of Purity in the Shimmering Cold

Snowflakes twirl like dancers in flight,
Each one unique, a delicate sight.
They blanket the ground in soft, white grace,
Transforming the world to a magical space.

Children giggle, their laughter rings clear,
Building snowmen, spreading holiday cheer.
Winter's ballad plays, serene and sweet,
As nature dons her frosty, white sheet.

Frills of Ice on Nature’s Canvas

On windows, crystals form intricate lace,
Nature’s brush paints with exquisite grace.
Icicles hang like jewels in the sun,
Each moment a treasure, a frozen run.

Branches bow low under the heavy weight,
The world is silenced as night grows late.
Hoarfrost glimmers under the pale moon,
A winter's whisper, a soft, sweet tune.

Light and Shadow in a Frozen Symphony

The contrast of sun on fields of white,
Creates a dance of shadow and light.
Morning glows softly on icy streams,
Awakening beauty, igniting dreams.

Whispers of wind weave through the trees,
Carrying tales of the winter's freeze.
In this frozen realm, I find my way,
In the light and the dark, I choose to stay.

Frozen Whispers of the Sleeping Earth

Beneath the snow, the secrets lie,
A silent breath, a gentle sigh.
The world wrapped tight in frosty breath,
Awaits the day that ends its death.

Icicles drip from branches bare,
While winter's cloak is everywhere.
Each whisper soft, a tale untold,
Of life beneath the chill so bold.

With every flake, a story flows,
In winter's grasp, the silence grows.
The earth holds tight its dreams asleep,
In frozen whispers, secrets keep.

Moonlight glimmers on the white,
A canvas pure, a tranquil sight.
Nature's breath, a hushed embrace,
In slumber's grip, a peaceful place.

So listen close to frozen dreams,
Within the chill, the silence teems.
For in this still and slumbered oak,
The heart of earth begins to hope.

Enchanted Windows of Winter Light

Through frosted panes, the daylight streams,
A magic world where sunlight gleams.
Each ray a brush of golden hue,
Painting warmth on the winter blue.

The breath of frost on glass so clear,
Reflects the beauty lingering near.
In each small shard, a tale unfolds,
Of winter's grip and stories told.

Sparkling edges, a crystal frame,
Nature’s art, a vibrant claim.
These windows whisper of the past,
Of fleeting moments, ever cast.

As night descends, the stars will glow,
Through every window, newly show.
An enchanting dance of shadows play,
In winter's clutch, where dreams may sway.

So gaze upon the wonders bright,
In each reflection, pure delight.
The warmth of love, a guiding light,
Enchanted windows, winter's might.

Crystal Feathers Floating on Air

A flurry drifts, so soft, so light,
The crystal feathers take to flight.
They glide on breezes, free and fair,
Adorn the sky with frosted flair.

In swirling paths of white they weave,
A tapestry that winter leaves.
Each one a gem that softly glows,
A dance of nature, winter's prose.

They catch the sun in fleeting gleam,
Translucent hints of nature’s dream.
Each flutter soft begins to twirl,
A chorus of the snowy whirl.

Upon the wind, a gentle song,
Where crystal feathers float along.
They whisper tales of frosty nights,
And serenade the stars' delights.

So watch them drift, a fragile sight,
These fleeting wonders take to flight.
In every swirl, a silent prayer,
For dreams that dance upon the air.

The Art of Winter’s Frozen Palette

On nature's canvas, cold and wide,
A masterpiece where colors bide.
The white of snow, the blue of sky,
A tranquil spread where dreams can lie.

Frosted branches, a silver hue,
Each crystal branch, a work of view.
The shadows play, the light expands,
Creating magic across this land.

With gentle strokes, the seasons blend,
In winter’s grasp, where time won't bend.
The palette rich with every shade,
A masterpiece that won’t soon fade.

From whispered breaths to icy sparks,
Each corner holds its hidden marks.
The art of winter, pure and true,
A world transformed in chilly blue.

So stand and gaze at winter's sheet,
Where silence echoes, and dreams meet.
In every corner, beauty's sought,
The art of winter, softly wrought.

Crafting Whispers in Frost and Mist

In shadows soft, where frost does cling,
Whispers dance on winter's wing.
Each breath a tale, each sigh a spark,
In silence deep, we leave our mark.

The trees adorned in crystal lace,
As nature's breath finds gentle pace.
A world reborn in icy hues,
In every step, the dream ensues.

With every step, the snowflakes fall,
A tapestry, a winter's call.
The echoes of the past resound,
In frosted air, our hopes are found.

Mists of dreams in twilight glow,
Intertwined with tales we know.
In every heart, the chill of night,
Whispers weave a veil of light.

Awake we stand, our spirits high,
Beneath the vast and endless sky.
Crafting warmth in winter's kiss,
In frozen realms, we find our bliss.

An Ode to the Icy Altitudes

High above where eagles soar,
The icy peaks, forevermore.
A realm where silence reigns supreme,
In crystal air, we chase a dream.

The winds they sing a bitter tune,
Beneath the watchful, silver moon.
Majestic, bold, the mountains rise,
Their majesty a sweet surprise.

Each snow-kissed slope tells tales of old,
The whispered legends, brave and bold.
In sparkling snow, our spirits leap,
An ode to heights, the world so deep.

Through valleys low and canyons wide,
We seek the thrill, the icy glide.
Each gasp of air, a taste of life,
In these altitudes, there is no strife.

So raise a glass to peaks so grand,
To icy wonders across the land.
In every heartbeat, in every cheer,
An ode to heights, forever near.

Reflections of Dreams on Frozen Wings

In twilight's hush where secrets lie,
Dreams take flight like birds that fly.
Upon the ice, reflections gleam,
In frozen air, we chase our dream.

Through chilly winds, the whispers glide,
Echoes of hope we cannot hide.
Each shimmering glance a story spun,
In the heart of winter, we are one.

With wings of frost, the spirits dance,
In every pause, there lies a chance.
To weave our tales in silver shades,
On frozen wings, our joy cascades.

The world stands still, a moment caught,
In icy breath, our battles fought.
We linger here, the magic grows,
In stillness deep, our longing shows.

So take my hand as we ascend,
On frozen wings, our hearts will blend.
Together we'll chase the northern lights,
In dreams of warmth on frosty nights.

Shards of Light on a Frozen Pond

Shards of light shine bright and clear,
Reflecting dreams from far and near.
A frozen world, so cold and white,
Holds the whispers of the night.

Beneath the surface, secrets lie,
With each soft breath, the ice will sigh.
Glimmers dance on crystal plains,
Nature's art, it softly reigns.

Trees stand tall in silent grace,
Wrapped in winter's cold embrace.
Moonbeams play on icy glass,
As shadows shift and moments pass.

Life beneath awaits the thaw,
While silence speaks without a flaw.
A tranquil scene, both beautiful,
In frozen time, forever full.

Whispering Glimmers at Dawn

Whispering glimmers break the dark,
As dawn ignites with every spark.
Soft hues blend in gentle rays,
Caressing earth in warming plays.

Butterflies flutter, wings like lace,
In the tender, waking space.
Morning dew glistens on each blade,
Nature's beauty unafraid.

Birds rise up with sweet refrain,
Their melodies erase the pain.
Each note a promise, bold and bright,
Awakening the world to light.

Clouds drift softly, a waking sigh,
As colors melt across the sky.
Whispers of hope in every beam,
In the dawn, we find our dream.

Echoes of a Frostbitten Evening

Echoes whisper through the trees,
Carried gently by the breeze.
Frostbitten air, sharp and clear,
Holds the whispers we long to hear.

Beneath the stars, the night is still,
Nature's pulse, a quiet thrill.
Moonlight bathes the world in white,
A timeless dance of dark and light.

Footsteps crunch on frosty ground,
In solitude, where peace is found.
Shadows stretch with each cool breath,
An evening rich with quiet depth.

Time dissolves in silver gleam,
As echoes fade, we chase our dream.
Each moment holds the winter's grace,
In this night, we find our place.

Glistening Patterns on a Hidden Lake

Glistening patterns catch the eye,
On a hidden lake where whispers lie.
Ripples dance as breezes play,
In secret worlds, the echoes sway.

Sunlight pierces through the trees,
Painting gold on tranquil seas.
Smooth reflections mirror skies,
A canvas where the spirit flies.

Fish dart swiftly beneath the glow,
In depths where silent secrets flow.
Nature holds a sacred space,
In every curve, in every grace.

Leaves drift softly without a sound,
As time dissolves without a bound.
Glistening patterns, a fleeting muse,
In this haven, we choose to lose.

Crystal-Crowned Pines Under the Dawn

In the morning light they stand,
Draped in crystals, white and grand.
Soft whispers of the waking breeze,
Dance among their bended knees.

A canvas bright of emerald hue,
Outlined by frost, a brilliant view.
Each branch a tale, a silent song,
Of nature's grace where we belong.

As rays of sun break through the chill,
The quiet woods, alive, they thrill.
With gentle hues of pink and gold,
A new day's story, yet untold.

Beneath the boughs, a world so pure,
Each moment fleeting, yet secure.
In harmony they reach the skies,
Crystal-crowned beneath sunrise.

As light cascades through branches bare,
We find a truth, a tranquil care.
In this embrace, we breathe anew,
Crystal-crowned pines, we stand with you.

Petals Cradled in a Frozen Embrace

Beneath the snow, the petals lie,
In whispered dreams, they quietly sigh.
Fragrant memories trapped in frost,
Reminders of warmth, they thought they lost.

Each bloom a tale of summer's cheer,
Preserved in time, yet held so dear.
A blanket soft as silence falls,
Embracing blooms in crystal walls.

Nature's touch, both cruel and kind,
In frozen depths, life lingers blind.
Yet hope awakens with the thaw,
As spring returns, it stirs in awe.

So here they rest, in slumber deep,
Awaiting sunlight's warmest sweep.
Petals breathe, though wrapped in white,
Cradled close, they hold the light.

Their vibrant hues, though far away,
Will soon return, come bright of day.
In frozen embrace, they patiently wait,
For warmth to crack their frosty fate.

Frost-Sculpted Beauty of a New Dawn

As winter's breath paints all anew,
A masterpiece of white and blue.
Each crystal flake, a fleeting art,
A canvas crafted, a frozen heart.

Stillness reigns, the world aglow,
With diamond dust, a gentle show.
In every corner, beauty sprawls,
Frost-sculpted dreams on nature's walls.

The trees, adorned with icy lace,
Stand tall and proud, in silent grace.
Their branches sway to morning's song,
A tender tune where all belong.

With every ray, a spark ignites,
Breaking through cold, inviting lights.
A new dawn dawns, hope intertwined,
In frost-sculpted beauty, love we find.

As shadows lift, the world awakes,
In sparkling light, our hearts it makes.
Embracing warmth, we step outside,
To dance with dawn, arms open wide.

Shards of Light in the Cold Embrace

In winter's grasp, the world is still,
Soft shadows creep, the air a chill.
Yet in the silence, whispers glow,
Shards of light on newly-fallen snow.

Each crystal glints, a magic spark,
Illuminating paths so dark.
They guide our way through frosty air,
A shimmering trail, beyond compare.

Beneath the sky so vast and wide,
We find our strength, our hearts abide.
In chilly arms, we face the day,
Shards of light show us the way.

As time hangs on, each moment glows,
With every breath, a spirit grows.
In cold embrace, we feel alive,
With shards of light, our hopes arrive.

Together, we can brave the frost,
In every loss, there's beauty tossed.
So hand in hand, we find our trust,
In shards of light, our love's a must.

Shimmering Echoes in the Stillness

In the quiet, whispers dwell,
Softly ringing like a bell.
Moonlight dances on the lake,
Casting shadows, dreams awake.

Rippling sounds through night's embrace,
Every echo leaves a trace.
Gentle breezes weave their song,
In this stillness, we belong.

Murmurs of the world outside,
In this peace we can confide.
Moments glimmer, then they fade,
Yet the heart is unafraid.

Stars may twinkle, stars may glow,
In the silence, time moves slow.
Crickets chirp their lullabies,
Underneath the velvet skies.

Every whisper, every sigh,
Forms a tapestry nearby.
In this shimmering, tranquil space,
We find solace, love, and grace.

Winter’s Breath and Sparkling Prison

Frosted windows, a chilly sigh,
Snowflakes dance as they drift by.
Winter's breath, a frosty kiss,
Hiding warmth in every bliss.

Icicles hang like crystal longs,
Nature sings its quiet songs.
Glistening fields, a frozen sea,
Wrapped in white, so wild and free.

Footprints pressed in warm embrace,
Whispers of a softer place.
In this prison, cold and bright,
Dreams take flight in the moonlight.

Branches bare, yet life remains,
Underneath, the heart sustains.
In the stillness, peace is found,
A magical, enchanting sound.

Winter's breath, it holds us tight,
In its depths, we find our light.
Sparkling prisons, cold and clear,
Within, we shed every fear.

Glinting Crystals on a Silver Pendant

Light cascades from shining stones,
Whispers of forgotten tones.
Crystals glint with each soft glance,
In their presence, dreams enhance.

Silver threads weave through the night,
Casting shadows, catching light.
Every sparkle tells a tale,
Of hopes and dreams that never fail.

Adornment glows with secret grace,
In each facet, love's embrace.
Time stands still as visions spin,
In these jewels, the heart begins.

Echoed laughter, silent cheer,
Whispers that we hold so dear.
Life’s mosaic, bright and grand,
Reflects the touch of a gentle hand.

In the pendant's gleaming heart,
Shimmers stories set apart.
Glinting crystals, memories blend,
Forever young, they never end.

Serenity Under a Glacial Whisper

Beneath the frost, the world is still,
In every breath, a gentle thrill.
Glacial whispers softly flow,
Calming waves of winter's glow.

Mountains cradle icy streams,
In the silence, we find dreams.
Frozen gardens, white and pure,
Wrap us in their cool allure.

Breath of winter in the air,
Every moment stripped and bare.
Serenity, a quiet hold,
In the chill, our hearts unfold.

Softly nestled, hearts beat slow,
In this magic, time won't go.
Nature's stillness, pure and wide,
In its arms, we safely bide.

Underneath the stars above,
We discover winter's love.
Glacial whispers, sweet and bright,
Guide us through the frosty night.

Glimmering Shadows of Chill and Calm

In the quiet of the night,
Whispers dance with the frost,
Glimmering shadows take flight,
In stillness, we find what is lost.

Beneath the silver moonlight,
Dreams flutter with grace,
Echoes of laughter ignite,
Warming this frozen place.

Time slows to a gentle hum,
As cold nips at our heels,
In this moment, we become,
The truth that the heart reveals.

With each breath, the air glows bright,
Painting the world in hue,
Glimmering shadows unite,
In a symphony, pure and true.

Together we walk, hand in hand,
Beneath skies draped in stars,
In the chill, we gently stand,
Finding warmth in who we are.

Encased Dreams Beneath the Ice

Frozen whispers in the air,
Encased dreams softly sigh,
A world enchanted, beyond compare,
Where hopes and wishes lie.

Underneath the icy glaze,
Visions swirl in quiet pools,
As daylight starts to fade,
In this realm, nobody rules.

Stars twinkle in the deep,
Guarding secrets tucked away,
In the silence, they safely sleep,
Awaiting the break of day.

With each crystal, stories unfold,
Writing on the frozen ground,
In this wonderland of gold,
Magic in stillness is found.

So let us tread with gentle feet,
Upon this shimmering seam,
Where encased dreams meet,
And dance in the light of the dream.

Pearls of Winter's Breath

Amidst the chill of winter's breath,
Soft pearls glisten on the trees,
A beauty that whispers of life and death,
Carried on the coldest breeze.

Each flake glimmers like a star,
A delicate dance in the night,
It travels near and far,
Filling the world with pure delight.

Beneath the weight of silent snow,
Nature's canvas gleams and shines,
Where every pearl is sure to know,
Of stories told through ancient lines.

In the stillness, we find our peace,
Drawing close to warmth and fire,
As winter’s wonders never cease,
In a realm that inspires.

So let us gather each soft pearl,
With the magic of winter’s song,
In this enchanting, frozen whirl,
Where dreams and wonders belong.

Twinkling Secrets of Frosted Nights

Beneath a veil of frosted white,
Twinkling secrets softly play,
In the embrace of the peaceful night,
Where stars whisper and sway.

Every breath creates a mist,
In the quiet, hearts align,
Holding tight to moments kissed,
By magic, pure, divine.

Silhouettes of trees stand tall,
Against the darkened sky,
In this serene, enchanting thrall,
We find the reason why.

With each step, the world awakes,
Crystals sparkling in the light,
In the dance that winter makes,
Treasures hidden from our sight.

So gather close, as wonders bloom,
In each soft twinkle, take your flight,
Where love will always find the room,
In twinkling secrets of frosted nights.

Winter’s Palette of Glimmer and Glow

A silver hush falls softly down,
In quiet corners, whispers drown.
The pale blue sky begins to gleam,
While frosted trees hold nature's dream.

Crimson berries cling to boughs,
While winter's breath makes nature bow.
Through crystal flakes, the world ignites,
In this serene, enchanting night.

A canvas painted, white and bright,
With strokes of amber, gold, and light.
Each draping snowflake, unique flight,
A winter's palette glimmers right.

Stars above in velvet shrouds,
Twinkling softly, they are proud.
As shadows dance upon the ground,
In winter’s glow, pure peace is found.

Through icy trails, the soft winds sing,
As nature rests, preparing Spring.
In gleaming glow, the world is bound,
In winter's heart, pure joy is found.

Shivers of Light Across a Frosted Heart

Beneath the chill of evening's veil,
A frosted heart begins to wail.
In silver light, the shadows play,
As winter's chill consumes the day.

Each breath released, a cloud of mist,
The warmth of love, sweetly kissed.
Soft whispers travel on the breeze,
A dance of hope among the trees.

Crystals form on window panes,
While memory calls like gentle rains.
Shivers of light brush past my skin,
Awakening warmth that lies within.

As twinkling stars grace the night sky,
Dreams take flight, and soars on high.
In frosted stillness, a fire starts,
Illuminating a frozen heart.

With every flake, a story told,
Of winter's magic, bright and bold.
Through prisms of light that twirl and sway,
A frosted heart finds warmth today.

Reflective Hues on the Icebound Stream

Still waters glimmer under frost,
In nature’s beauty, we are lost.
Reflective hues like shattered glass,
Each layer holds the winter’s past.

Golden rays through branches seep,
Awakening secrets, once asleep.
The crisp air dances, full of grace,
Embracing all in nature's space.

Every ripple, a tale unfolds,
Of quiet moments, truth beholds.
Icebound dreams whisper soft and low,
In tranquil depths, where waters flow.

Soft shadows play on frozen ground,
Nature's beauty, all around.
In the embrace of winter’s dream,
We find our peace on the still stream.

As twilight paints the world anew,
In softest gray and deepest blue,
Reflective hues in tranquil gleam,
Awaken hearts in winter's scheme.

The Twist of Time in Frosted Patterns

Time bends softly in the cold,
Frosted patterns, stories told.
Each flake a whisper, fleeting grace,
In winter's embrace, we find our place.

Nature's brush dips in the freeze,
Creating art in frosted trees.
The icy wind, a timeless tune,
Sings softly underneath the moon.

With every crack, each brittle sound,
A world reborn, with magic found.
The twist of time in frosted art,
Whispers secrets to the heart.

Moments linger, then drift away,
Like passing clouds on a gray day.
Yet in the stillness, we can see,
Frosted patterns, eternity.

As dawn arrives, the light will weave,
New stories for us to believe.
In winter's chill, time holds us tight,
Within its folds, a pure delight.

Gemstone Fragments of Chilling Air

Gemstone fragments twinkle bright,
Caught in the stillness of the night.
Whispers dance on frosty breath,
Each crystal echoing nature's death.

A moonlit glow plays on the ground,
As shadows in the silence surround.
Frozen smiles in a silent prayer,
Softly linger in the chilling air.

The stars above shine cold and clear,
Illuminating all we hold dear.
Every glimmer a story told,
In this winter’s gentle fold.

Winds weave tales of ancient lore,
Running fingers on the icy shore.
Nature hums its quiet song,
In harmony, we all belong.

So let the frost embrace my soul,
In the gemstone glow, I am whole.
With every breath, the night concedes,
To the beauty where silence breeds.

The Frosted Veil of Twilight Dreams

Twilight spills its colors bright,
As day surrenders to the night.
A frosted veil begins to rise,
Enshrouding all beneath the skies.

Dreams drift softly on the air,
Wrapped in silver, light as prayer.
Each star above, a whispered thought,
In the stillness, gently sought.

Misty tendrils creep and curl,
In the dance of day’s last twirl.
The world transforms in muted hues,
As night unveils its tranquil views.

With every shadow, magic weaves,
In the twilight, the heart believes.
Stories linger, yet unsaid,
Beneath the frosted dreams we tread.

As dreams take flight under starlit skies,
Hope ignites with each sunrise.
In the embrace of night so deep,
Awake the treasures we keep.

Frosted Latticework on Nature's Canvas

Nature's canvas frozen tight,
Latticework of pure delight.
Patterns woven with icy grace,
Beauty shines in every space.

Each twig adorned with crystal lace,
Reflecting winter's sweet embrace.
Branches arch, a frosty crown,
In this wonderland renowned.

Drifting flakes like whispered dreams,
Glimmer softly in moonbeams.
Every flake a tale unfolds,
In the chill, the mystery holds.

A serenity in cold repose,
Where time stands still and silence grows.
Each breath a cloud in crisp, still air,
Frosted beauty everywhere.

So let us wander through this scene,
Among the white and shades of green.
In nature's art, we find our peace,
As winter's charm will never cease.

Icy Lace Adorning Silent Meadows

Icy lace steps into view,
Adorning meadows, fresh and new.
A soft white blanket, nature's hold,
Whispers secrets yet untold.

Across the fields where silence reigns,
Each frost-kissed blade, a work that gains.
In the hush of morning light,
The world transforms, pure and bright.

With every footfall, a crunching sound,
In this winter's realm, joy is found.
A canvas stretched, so vast, so wide,
In icy lace, dreams can bide.

Underneath the pale blue skies,
Nature breathes with quiet sighs.
Each crystal spark, a moment's glance,
In the stillness, hearts can dance.

So let us wander, hand in hand,
Through this enchanted, frozen land.
In icy lace, old tales revive,
In silent meadows, we're alive.

Frosted Murmurs in the Quiet Woods

In shadows deep where whispers flow,
The frosted boughs in moonlight glow.
Each step a crackle, crisp and clear,
Nature's secrets gently near.

A rustle stirs beneath the snow,
As silent creatures come and go.
The pine trees sway with tranquil grace,
Embracing peace in this still place.

The stars peek down through branches high,
While snowflakes dance like dreams that fly.
A hush envelops every sound,
In this enchanting winter ground.

With every breath, the chill arrives,
Where frozen whispers keep alive.
Magic lingers on the breeze,
Inviting hearts to feel at ease.

So in these woods, the calm remains,
Wrapped in winter's soft refrains.
The frosted murmurs intertwine,
In nature's song, pure and divine.

Sparkling Horizons of Icy Dreams

Dawn breaks gently on icy plains,
A canvas bright where sunlight reigns.
Each crystal shard begins to gleam,
Awakening the world from dream.

Mountains rise with jeweled caps,
Reflecting light in silver maps.
Beyond the edge where shadows play,
Lies beauty born from night to day.

The frozen lakes a mirror show,
Capturing all the warmth and glow.
With every ripple, magic flows,
As spirit of the winter glows.

Winds whisper secrets, soft as lace,
Through icy realms and quiet space.
Each breath of frost, a tale well spun,
In sparkling hues, the day begun.

So let us wander, hand in hand,
Through sparkling dreams in this vast land.
With hearts aglow and spirits bright,
We chase the horizons, pure delight.

Misty Secrets of the Frozen Glen

Through the hush of morning's veil,
Lies a glen where tales prevail.
Misty secrets softly weave,
In shadows where the heart believes.

Whispers rise from frozen streams,
Telling stories wrapped in dreams.
Beneath the frost, the earth does sigh,
In tender breaths, the memories lie.

Tall trees stand like sentinels,
Guarding stories, weaving spells.
A quiet dance of mist and light,
Revealing wonders out of sight.

Footsteps trace the winding path,
Lead us where the shadows bathe.
In twilight's glow, the spirits gleam,
In misty whispers, feel the dream.

So linger here in frozen grace,
And lose yourself in nature's embrace.
For in this glen, the secrets flow,
A whispered truth in silent snow.

Glistening Ghosts in the Morning Mist

When dawn unveils the frosty ground,
Glistening ghosts in silence found.
They dance and flutter, soft and light,
In the hushed embrace of pale daylight.

The world adorned in silver sheen,
Every edge and curve serene.
As mist rolls in like whispered sighs,
The spirits weave where silence lies.

Among the trees, their shadows sigh,
Creating tales that drift and fly.
Each breath a whisper of the past,
In morning's touching, gentle cast.

Through tangled brambles, soft and wild,
Nature cradles every child.
The glistening ghosts, they twirl and spin,
In harmony where dreams begin.

So take a moment, breathe it in,
In the morning mist where hope begins.
For glistening ghosts shall ever roam,
In every heart, they find a home.

The Dance of Frosted Petals

Beneath the moon’s soft glow, they twirl,
Frosted petals in a nightly whirl.
With every gust, they sway in trance,
Nature's beauty in a fleeting dance.

A garden dressed in shimmering white,
Hush of the night, the world feels right.
Whispers of beauty, a silent hymn,
As dawn approaches, the light grows dim.

Gentle breezes spin them high,
Like dreams awakened under the sky.
Each petal tells a tale of grace,
In the stillness, we find our place.

Beneath the stars, the petals gleam,
Nature's artwork, a tranquil dream.
Time stands still in this frosted waltz,
Every moment, a soft heart's pulse.

So let us watch this dance unfold,
In frosted petals, stories told.
In the whispers of the night, we are one,
In the fleeting beauty, life’s begun.

Diamond Dust on Silent Streams

Glittering gems on water's face,
Silent streams in nature’s embrace.
Morning sunlight spills like wine,
Casting diamonds where waters twine.

Ripples whisper through the hush,
A symphony in nature's rush.
Each reflection, a moment caught,
In the calm, a world of thought.

Beneath the bridge where willows weep,
The secrets of the waters creep.
Dancing light on every wave,
Echoes of life, stories brave.

As shadows lengthen, colors fade,
Still the stream, in silence laid.
A tapestry of nature’s art,
In diamond dust, we play our part.

In twilight’s glow, the world slows down,
A peaceful hush envelops the town.
On silent streams, dreams take flight,
Wrapped in magic of the night.

Frosty Kisses on a Wooden Rail

Morning breaks with frosty breath,
Whispers soft, like life and death.
On wooden rails, the frost takes hold,
Kisses glisten, quiet and bold.

Each slat adorned with icy lace,
A frosty touch, nature’s grace.
The air is crisp, a gentle bite,
In stillness found, morning’s light.

Birds chirp softly in the trees,
While breezes carry whispers, a tease.
Frosty jewels on a forgotten place,
Where time feels slow, where memories trace.

As sunlight warms the world anew,
The wooden rail holds stories true.
Each chilly kiss, a note of time,
In every moment, we find our rhyme.

So let us wander, hand in hand,
On frosty paths through winter land.
With every step, our hearts will sail,
In the magic of this wooden rail.

Whispering Hail in Starlit Shadows

In starlit shadows, the night unfolds,
Whispers of hail, secrets untold.
Each drop a story, soft and small,
A gentle dance, a moonlit call.

Beneath the night's ethereal grace,
Hail like diamonds, an intricate lace.
They patter softly on the ground,
A melody of calm, profound.

In every corner, whispers sigh,
Underneath the vast, velvet sky.
Nature's heartbeat, a soothing sound,
In whispers of hail, love is found.

With every sparkle, dreams ignite,
In shadows deep, the world feels right.
A quiet magic weaves through the air,
Enveloping hearts in tender care.

So as the night whispers, let us stay,
In starlit shadows, come what may.
For in this moment, we live, we breathe,
In the hail's soft kiss, our hearts believe.

Ethereal Crystals Beneath the Darkness

In shadows gleam the fractured light,
Ethereal crystals shining bright.
They whisper tales of ages old,
Where secrets dance, and dreams unfold.

Beneath the weight of endless night,
Pure wonders twinkle, pure delight.
Each shard a dream, a world apart,
Igniting sparks within the heart.

Through veils of mist, the visions glide,
In silent halls where spirits bide.
A symphony of light and shade,
A tapestry of stars displayed.

With every glance, a story blooms,
In moonlit realms, where silence looms.
The darkness holds its subtle grace,
In crystal veils, we find our place.

Ethereal beauty, softly cast,
In fleeting moments, shadows passed.
With open hearts, we dare to dream,
In crystal realms where starlight gleams.

Winter's Lament in Glistening White

The world is wrapped in sheets of snow,
A quiet hush, where cold winds blow.
Branches bow beneath the weight,
Of winter’s touch, both cruel and great.

Silent echoes fill the air,
A ghostly dance, a crisp despair.
Each flake that falls, a whispered sigh,
As winter wraps the earth to die.

In twilight’s glow, the shadows play,
As daylight dims in soft decay.
A fleeting warmth, the sun retreats,
While frost and ice claim winter’s seats.

The fire's glow, a heart’s embrace,
In hidden nooks, we find our place.
Yet in the chill, a beauty lies,
In winter's song, the heart complies.

With every breath, a cloud of mist,
The world transformed, a silvered tryst.
In glistening white, we feel the weight,
Of winter’s night, a softened fate.

Fractured Beauty in the Cold

Beneath the frost, the blooms lay low,
Fractured beauty, in icy flow.
Each petal kissed by winter's hand,
A frozen script across the land.

The bitter wind, a haunting song,
Reminds us where we once belonged.
Yet beauty holds its silent grace,
In every line, in every trace.

Icicles hang like crystal tears,
Memories bound by chilled frontiers.
Within the cold, resilience grows,
From fractured dreams, new life bestows.

The bleakness wraps the world in gray,
Yet in the heart, a spark will sway.
For in the shadows, light will break,
And beauty blooms from every ache.

So let the frost embrace the night,
In fractured beauty, hope takes flight.
For even in the coldest space,
Love finds a way, and dreams embrace.

Frozen Serenade of the Night

In frozen fields, the silence reigns,
A serenade of soft refrains.
Where starlight glimmers on the frost,
And every moment feels like lost.

The moon hangs low, a silver dream,
As whispers float on chilly stream.
Each breath a melody, so sweet,
In night’s embrace, our hearts find beat.

The winding paths, in shadows dressed,
Invite lost souls to find their rest.
With every step, the world awakes,
To frozen songs that twilight makes.

Ethereal notes in darkened skies,
Guide us through where the magic lies.
The symphony of night unfolds,
In frozen dance, the heart beholds.

So let us sway to winter's tune,
‘Neath stars that glimmer, ‘neath the moon.
In frozen lands, where dreams unite,
We find our peace in the cold night.

Whispers of Ice in the Morning Light

Snowflakes dance in gentle breeze,
Softly falling with such ease.
Morning light begins to glow,
Whispers of ice in the snow.

Branches creak, a silent tune,
Beneath the watchful silver moon.
Frosty patterns on window panes,
Nature's art through cold remains.

Footsteps crunch on frozen ground,
In the stillness, peace is found.
A breath of chill within the air,
Quiet beauty everywhere.

In the distance, mountains rise,
Kissed by dawn's soft, golden sighs.
Whispers linger, soft and bright,
In the warmth of morning light.

Shattered Silence of Winter Mornings

In the hush of winter's morn,
Silence reigns, a day reborn.
Crystal shards reflect the sky,
Echoes of a soft goodbye.

Snowflakes spiral, twirl, and dive,
In this stillness, we arrive.
Each breath visible, crisp and clear,
Shattered silence, all we hear.

Footprints linger on the way,
Tracing stories of the day.
Every sound, a memory,
Frozen time, locked history.

Sunlight spills on frosty ground,
Gold and silver swirl around.
In this moment, heartbeats sync,
Winter's magic makes us think.

With each heartbeat, life awakes,
In the quiet, nature shakes.
Shattered silence, pure delight,
Winter’s gift, a world so bright.

Luminous Tendrils on Frozen Glass

Patterns weave on windows fair,
Luminous tendrils twisting there.
Frosty fingers trace their dance,
Nature's work, a fleeting chance.

Through the pane, the world glows bright,
Softened edges meet the light.
A canvas painted, pure and fine,
In frozen art, the stars align.

Morning breaks with gentle grace,
Illuminating every space.
Every breath a whispered prayer,
In this moment, we are rare.

Tendrils shimmer, catch the dawn,
As the day begins to draw on.
In this stillness, beauty found,
Frozen magic all around.

Fleeting visions, a frozen dream,
Glassy surfaces softly gleam.
Luminous tendrils, fleeting glance,
In winter's grip, we find romance.

Ethereal Shards Beneath the Moon

Underneath the silver glow,
Ethereal shards begin to show.
Crisp and clear in moonlight's grace,
A shimmering, enchanted space.

Each flake tells a story old,
Of memories in whispers told.
Caught in time, they softly gleam,
Reflecting every tender dream.

The night unfolds, a velvet shroud,
Embracing whispers from the crowd.
In the stillness, hearts unite,
Beneath the spell of starry night.

Frozen landscapes, precious sights,
Dancing softly in the lights.
Ethereal moments, fleeting grace,
In the coolness, we find our place.

Moonlit paths, where shadows play,
Guiding wanderers on their way.
Ethereal shards, a moment's kiss,
In winter's night, we find our bliss.

Midnight Silence Wrapped in Frost

In the stillness, whispers roam,
Beneath the moon's soft, silver dome.
Frosted fields lay hushed and white,
Embraced by the calm of the night.

Stars glisten bright in the skies,
While shadows twist, then softly rise.
Each breath released, a misty plume,
As night unfolds its tranquil gloom.

Trees stand guard, their branches bare,
Crystals shimmer in chilled air.
Nature sleeps, yet dreams takes flight,
Wrapped in silence, wrapped in light.

Footsteps crunch on the frozen ground,
Echoes linger, softly sound.
With every step, a tale we weave,
In midnight's hush, we too believe.

And as the dawn begins to creep,
The world awakes from frosty sleep.
Yet in our hearts, that silence stays,
A memory of those frost-kissed days.

Nature’s Jewels on Glistening Grasses

Morning dew, like diamonds shine,
Adorning leaves in pure design.
Each blade holds a tiny glow,
A treasure trove, a gentle show.

Sunlight dances, warm and bright,
Painting dreams in hues of light.
Nature's brush, with softest hand,
Casts magic on this verdant land.

Bees hum softly, busy and free,
Fluttering near the jasmine tree.
Colors burst, life’s vivid song,
In this world where we belong.

Birds take flight, a fleeting sight,
Chasing shadows, taking flight.
With open wings, they paint the sky,
While whispers of the wind pass by.

Every petal, each fragrant bloom,
Fills the air with sweet perfume.
Nature shines in every glance,
An endless, joyful, vibrant dance.

Winter’s Heartbeat in a Crystal Shell

Amidst the chill, a rhythm flows,
Winter's heartbeat softly knows.
In crystal shells, the world is caught,
Frozen whispers, warm thoughts sought.

Snowflakes drift like gentle sighs,
Falling softly from the skies.
Each flake dances, unique and pure,
In this hush, we find the cure.

Fires crackle in cozy homes,
As the wind through branches roams.
Warmth envelops, love takes hold,
In the heart of winter's fold.

Stars above, a distant choir,
Inspires dreams, ignites the fire.
Nature's pulse, a silent grace,
Winter’s heart knows every trace.

And as the dusk begins to blend,
With twilight’s charm, the night we send.
In crystal shells, our dreams confide,
Beneath the cosmos, we abide.

A Tapestry of Ice in the Winds

Winds weave tales in frosty threads,
Stitching wonders where nature spreads.
A tapestry in white and blue,
Covers the world with morning dew.

Branches laden, heavy with grace,
In winter's clutch, they find their place.
Each gust a whisper, soft and bright,
Painting joy in pure twilight.

Frozen rivers, still as glass,
Reflect the clouds as moments pass.
With every ripple, tales unfold,
In icy whispers, stories told.

Footsteps trace the silent ground,
In this frozen realm, peace is found.
Nature's breath, both wild and sweet,
Brings together all we greet.

So let us wander, hand in hand,
Through this wonderland so grand.
A tapestry woven, rich and fine,
In winter's arms, our hearts entwine.

Ethereal Ribbons in the Winter Breeze

Whispers weave through the silver pines,
A dance of shadows, soft and fine.
Caught in the breath of chilly air,
Ethereal ribbons, twisting with flair.

Snowflakes shimmer like fragile dreams,
Drifting gently on whispered screams.
Nature’s canvas, painted so bright,
A tapestry spun from purest white.

Branches cradled in frosty lace,
Timeless beauty found in this place.
Secrets held in the winter's breath,
Ethereal wonders, neither life nor death.

Each moment fleeting, yet deeply felt,
Warmth of the heart, though the air may melt.
As soft as the sigh of evening stars,
The ribbons of winter whisper in bars.

So let us dance in the frosted air,
In the embrace of a winter's prayer.
For within the chill, a spark ignites,
Ethereal ribbons, our souls take flight.

The Silhouette of Frosted Dreams

In the quiet hush of a winter night,
Silhouettes gather, feeling the light.
Frosted whispers dazzle the sky,
Dreams take shape, and gently sigh.

Moonlight kisses the icy streams,
Casting shadows on woven dreams.
A ballet of twinkles, bright and bold,
Stories of warmth quietly unfold.

Fragrant air, a hint of pine,
Echoes linger on the twilight line.
Every silhouette, a tale to tell,
In the heart of winter, we find our well.

Glistening echoes of laughter freeze,
In the realm where the heart's at ease.
The silhouette smiles, a gentle grace,
Frosted dreams in a cherished space.

Let us wade through the evening's chill,
Where shadows dance and time stands still.
Embrace the magic, let it gleam,
In the silhouette of frosted dreams.

A Kaleidoscope on the Icy Horizon

Colors blend in a canvas wide,
Icy horizons where wonders glide.
Fractured light, in patterns that play,
A kaleidoscope brightens the gray.

If you listen close, you'll hear a song,
Nature's chorus, where we belong.
Each note a splash on the frosty scene,
In a world of magic, vivid and keen.

Crystals twinkle, a spark of gold,
Secrets of winter, waiting to hold.
Mirrored moments, shifting through time,
In every breath, the universe rhymes.

Waltzing shadows across the land,
A dance of colors, eternally planned.
The icy horizon, a painter's delight,
A kaleidoscope glowing in the night.

So come take part in this visual thrill,
And let your spirit rise and spill.
For within this frame, eternity thrives,
A kaleidoscope where magic survives.

The Alchemy of Ice and Luminescence

In the hush of night, where shadows roam,
Ice transforms, creating a home.
Luminescence twinkles, a guiding spark,
Illuminating paths through the dark.

Crystals whisper secrets of old,
Stories of warmth in the bitter cold.
Nature's alchemy, a sacred blend,
Life and light forever transcend.

Glistening branches, touch of a hand,
Beneath the stars, we take a stand.
In this space where the ice meets light,
The heart ignites, burning so bright.

With each breath, we weave and mend,
Spaces where dreams and wonders lend.
Alchemy of ice, a wondrous dance,
Where luminescence sparks the chance.

So let us wander, hand in hand,
Through the realms where magic is planned.
In the glow of winter's embrace,
We find our place in time and space.

For in this beauty lies the truth,
The alchemy eternal, ageless youth.
Where ice meets light in a cosmic flight,
We journey forth into the night.

Enchanted Radiance of the Frosted Evening

Twilight cloaks the silent ground,
Softly whispers, gently found.
Stars awaken, crisp and bright,
Casting dreams in silver light.

Frosted branches gently sway,
Echoes of the fading day.
Moonlit shadows, midnight's grace,
In this calm, we find our place.

Every breath a clouded sigh,
Kissed by chill that wanders by.
Nature's hush, a sacred hymn,
In the night, the world grows dim.

Crystals sparkle on the breeze,
Each one nestled in the trees.
Whispers dance on frosty air,
Magic weaves with tender care.

Underneath this starlit dome,
Hearts awaken, finding home.
In this space, we feel alive,
Where the frozen dreams do thrive.

The Play of Light in a Crystal Covey

Morning breaks with golden hue,
Illuminating all anew.
Prisms caught in winter's weave,
Nature's art, a heart's reprieve.

Glitters dance on every edge,
Sparkling tales we now allege.
World transformed by sunlit rays,
Lost in moments, time decays.

Colors burst in canvas bright,
Shadows playing with the light.
In this cradle of pure bliss,
Each soft glance a fleeting kiss.

Harmony in colors blend,
Every shimmer, every bend.
Joyful echoes, laughter shared,
In this covey, souls are bared.

As the sun begins to rise,
Hope unfolds beneath the skies.
In a world that glows and gleams,
We find solace in our dreams.

Shimmering Hues across the Snowy Expanse

Across the fields, a blanket white,
Shimmering hues in morning light.
Gentle whispers, cool and clear,
Nature's canvas, bright and near.

Footprints mark the powdery floor,
Echoes of the tales before.
Sunshine mingles with the snow,
Painting everywhere we go.

Crimson berries peek through frost,
Wonders found, we thought were lost.
Laughter rolls like winter's breeze,
Fleeting moments, hearts at ease.

Glimmers dart like silver fish,
Touching souls with every wish.
In this realm, pure magic flows,
Among the beauty, our love grows.

With every turn, a spark ignites,
In the quiet, pure delights.
Snowy expanse, a world so wide,
In its embrace, we gently glide.

Glacial Breezes in a Dance of Light

Wind whispers secrets, pure and cold,
Carrying tales that time has told.
Glacial breezes sway and bend,
In the twilight, as day ends.

Light cascades on icy streams,
Shattering reflections, frosty dreams.
Weaving through the trees so tall,
In their grace, we hear the call.

Patterns form in icy lace,
Nature's dance, a fluid grace.
Every flake a story spun,
In the glow of setting sun.

Together swaying, shadows play,
As the night consumes the day.
In this moment, hearts ignite,
Beneath the stars, our souls take flight.

Glacial whispers, tender sighs,
Wrapped in warmth 'neath wintry skies.
In this dance where spirits rise,
We find love that never dies.

Icicles of Illumination

Hanging crystals, sharp and bright,
Glistening under soft moonlight.
Nature's art, a frozen stream,
Whispers secrets, soft as a dream.

Caught in time, the world stands still,
Breath of winter, a gentle chill.
Icicles dance in twilight's glow,
Each a story, each a flow.

Stars above, twinkling eyes,
Silent wonders fill the skies.
Frigid tales on winter's breath,
Eternal echoes, whispering death.

Frosty branches, shadows blend,
In this silence, heartbeats mend.
Twinkling lights, the night's embrace,
Icicles shine, a magic space.

In the stillness, calm unfolds,
Gentle warmth as daylight scolds.
Icicles melt, yet memories stay,
Marking nights of winter's play.

Chilled Whispers in the Moonlight

Moonlit rivers softly glide,
Chilled whispers, nature's pride.
Shadowed paths, secrets untold,
Each night brushes the world in gold.

Frozen echoes dance on air,
Caress of frost, a lover's care.
Bare branches sigh, they bend and sway,
In the stillness, dreams drift away.

Nightingale songs wrapped in ice,
Fleeting moments, like a dice.
Beneath the stars, a quiet plea,
For peace and hope, eternally.

Softly glimmers, lights in rows,
As twilight deepens, magic flows.
Chilled whispers weave through the night,
Painting shadows, pure delight.

In the moon's embrace, hearts entwine,
Silent wishes, pure and divine.
Chilled whispers in the moonlight's grace,
Soft as velvet, time's gentle embrace.

Frosted Petals and Shimmering Dreams

Frosted petals on the ground,
Whispers of beauty all around.
Shimmering dreams in winter's calm,
Nature's lullaby, a soothing balm.

Glistening fields, a blanket white,
Sparkling jewels in soft twilight.
Each petal holds a story's spark,
Memories woven in the dark.

Breath of winter, crisp and pure,
Silent moments, hearts secure.
The world transformed, a fairy tale,
Shimmering dreams through snowflakes sail.

Time is frozen in the night,
Petals glowing in silver light.
Frosted whispers, secrets shared,
In the beauty, hearts declared.

Shimmering dreams, a gentle flight,
Carried softly into the night.
Frosted petals, memories gleam,
In every heart, a winter dream.

Silver Veils of Winter's Breath

Silver veils haunt the quiet woods,
Soft as shadows, nature broods.
A touch of frost, a breath of light,
Dancing softly in the night.

Windswept whispers, secrets entwined,
In every branch, stories aligned.
Veils of silver, mystery's embrace,
Softly holding time's gentle pace.

Crimson berries, a dash of cheer,
Amidst the frost, hope appears.
Winter's breath, a painter's hand,
Spreading beauty across the land.

Beneath the stars, a world anew,
In silver veils, dreams come true.
Frosty kisses in the air,
Wrapped in magic, nothing compares.

The nightingale rests, the world at peace,
In silver veils, worries cease.
Winter's breath, a soft caress,
In nature's arms, we find our rest.

Twinkling Crystals of a Chilling Night

Under a blanket of starry delight,
Crystals glimmer, a mesmerizing sight.
The moon whispers secrets, soft and bright,
As dreams take flight in the chilly night.

Shadows dance upon the frosty ground,
Nature's beauty silently abounds.
Each breath a mist, where chill is found,
In this tranquil world, peace surrounds.

Pine trees adorned with silver lace,
Each branch a wonder, a crystal embrace.
The cold air tingles, a tender grace,
In the heart of winter, a soothing place.

Footprints fade in the shimmering snow,
Leaving tales of wanderers who go.
In the quiet night, the cold winds blow,
As twinkling crystals put on a show.

With every heartbeat, the night unfolds,
In whispers of magic, a story told.
The world wrapped in a shimmer of gold,
Twinkling crystals in the night's hold.

Frosty Imprints in the Quietude

Amidst the silence, a frosty trace,
Soft patterns emerge, a delicate grace.
Whispers of winter, time’s slow pace,
In this quietude, we find our place.

Nature sleeps under a crystal sheet,
Each breath releases a frosty beat.
In the calm of night, where shadows meet,
Frosty imprints beneath our feet.

The trees wear coats of sparkling frost,
In this serene world, nothing feels lost.
Every glint, a memory embossed,
In the glorious chill, we count the cost.

Footsteps fade in the soft white dust,
Leaving echoes of laughter and trust.
In frost’s embrace, we feel we must,
Celebrate the moments, as all things rust.

Under the stars, the night unfolds,
Frosty imprints of stories told.
In the quietude, love’s warmth enfolds,
As winter’s magic gently molds.

Threads of Light in the Winter's Shroud

Beneath the blanket of soft, white snow,
Threads of light in the dark we follow.
A dance of colors begins to glow,
As whispers of winter begin to flow.

In the hush of twilight, shadows play,
Moments unravel, drifting away.
Through icy branches, the stars will sway,
Threads of light guide us, come what may.

Skies painted with hues, a fleeting art,
Each ray a promise, a brand new start.
Wrapped in winter's tender heart,
We find the beauty in every part.

With every breath, a new canvas draws,
Impressions linger, time softly thaws.
In the shimmer of night, we find our cause,
Threads of light in winter's applause.

Underneath the moon's gentle embrace,
We chase the warmth in the cold's cold space.
As darkness yields, we find our place,
Threads of light weaving an endless grace.

The Mirror of Twilight’s Winter Glint

In twilight's embrace, the world does shine,
A mirror of magic, pure and divine.
Each flake of snow, a delicate sign,
Reflects the dreams that intertwine.

Through branches bare, a soft light seeps,
In whispers of winter, the quiet keeps.
With every moment, the heart leaps,
In the mirror of twilight, our spirit reaps.

Frost-kissed skies, a canvas so rare,
Where shadows blend with the crisp, cold air.
In this stillness, we find what’s fair,
The beauty of winter is always there.

The glint of stars in the evening’s fold,
Glimmers of silver, stories retold.
In the mirror of twilight, brave and bold,
We gather warmth as the night grows cold.

Through every breath, the world reflects,
A winter’s magic that softly connects.
Twilight's mirror, where the heart detects,
In its shimmering glow, love’s warmth evokes.

Radiant Veils of Morning Chill

The dawn unfolds its gentle hue,
A whisper soft, the night bids adieu.
Frosted branches glimmer bright,
As nature stirs from the cloak of night.

Sunrise pours a golden stream,
Awakening the world from dream.
Each breath a mist, a fleeting mark,
In the tranquil, glistening park.

Birds begin their morning song,
Their melodies sweet, enduring long.
Buds bloom under the warming ray,
Embracing the promise of the day.

Shadows shift and colors mix,
A dance of light, an enchanting fix.
Veils of morning, crisp and pure,
Wrap the world in a vibrant allure.

In this moment, time stands still,
A perfect pause, a gentle thrill.
Radiant veils in every breath,
Whispering tales of life and death.

Dancing Lights on an Icy Canvas

Underneath the moon’s bright gaze,
The world transforms in silvery haze.
Stars glitter like frozen dew,
Painting dreams in shimmering blue.

An icy canvas spread so wide,
Reflecting nature’s wondrous pride.
Lights twinkle in the frosty air,
A ballet of magic, pure and rare.

Footprints tell a story clear,
Of laughter shared, of warmth and cheer.
Children dance in joyful play,
With hearts aglow, they seize the day.

The night unfolds its secret grace,
As shadows twirl in a soft embrace.
Dancing lights, so wild and free,
Illuminate our memories.

In this frozen realm of bliss,
Every moment is pure happiness.
A canvas crafted by night's hand,
Where dreams and reality beautifully stand.

Shimmering Silence in a Winter's Tale

The world adorned in snowy white,
Whispers secrets through the night.
Every flake, a story told,
In the silence, dreams unfold.

Trees wear cloaks of sparkling frost,
In this beauty, none are lost.
A tranquil hush, the stillness deep,
Where winter's wonders softly creep.

Birds find solace in the cold,
Their songs a warmth, a heart of gold.
Nature breathes a silent sigh,
Underneath the vast, starry sky.

Footsteps crunched on snowy ground,
Echoes of life, a gentle sound.
In this shimmering, quiet veil,
Lies the magic of winter's tale.

Each moment lingers, pure and bright,
Wrapped in whispers of the night.
Shimmering silence takes its hold,
A winter story softly told.

Opalescent Mirrors of the Midnight Sky

Glistening stars like diamonds shine,
In the fabric of the night, divine.
The moon, a guardian of dreams,
Illuminates the world in beams.

Clouds drift like whispers, soft and light,
In opalescent hues, pure delight.
A canvas painted with cosmic grace,
Each twinkle holds a sacred space.

The nightingale sings to the moon,
A symphony of silken tune.
In the stillness, hearts unite,
Beneath the magic of the night.

Reflections dance in every eye,
As souls embrace the midnight sky.
Opalescent dreams in a gentle sway,
Guide us onward, night or day.

In this theater of stars and lore,
We find the peace we long for more.
Mirrors of time, they hold our fears,
Yet in their light, we shed our tears.

The Crystal Song of Winter Nights

Whispers of the frost in the air,
Crystals twinkle, stars unaware.
Moonlight dances on silvered trees,
A soft lullaby within the breeze.

Snowflakes flutter, gentle and white,
Wrapping the world in a blanket of light.
Echoes of silence, the night profound,
In this frozen haven, peace is found.

Each breath clouds like a fleeting dream,
Nighttime magic, soft as a seam.
The world suspended in time's embrace,
In winter's song, we find our place.

Stars blink softly, a celestial choir,
Illuminating paths we aspire.
With every heartbeat, the night unfolds,
A symphony whispered, a tale retold.

Let the cold wrap us in its grace,
In the crystal song, we find our space.
Winter nights hold secrets untold,
As dreams entwine with the beauty of cold.

Silken Hues of a Frozen Dawn

Beneath the sky, a canvas unfurls,
Silken hues in the morning swirls.
Pastel shades paint the snow so bright,
Awakening beauty, a breathtaking sight.

The chill of night whispers its retreat,
In soft, warm colors, the day is complete.
Frost-laden petals glimmer and gleam,
As sunlight stretches, a soft golden beam.

The breath of dawn, fresh and alive,
In nature's embrace, we truly thrive.
Awakening life in each tender ray,
As silken hues herald a brand new day.

Colors bleed softly around the trees,
A watercolor world swaying with ease.
Frozen moments captured in time,
In the heart of winter, nature’s prime.

The day breaks clear, washing shadows away,
With silken hues brightening our way.
In the stillness, a promise we see,
Of warmth returning, setting us free.

Frost-kissed Petals Under Starlit Skies

Petals shimmer with frost's gentle touch,
Under the vastness where dreams clutch.
Each flower whispers secrets of night,
Beneath the stars, it sparkles bright.

Moonlight caresses, tender and light,
Illuminating petals, a wondrous sight.
Nature’s artistry, a delicate scene,
In the glow of night, the world feels serene.

The fragrance lingers, soft and sweet,
A symphony played by the night’s heartbeat.
Frosty kisses in the cool, night air,
As starlit skies weave a spell, we share.

In this realm where the quiet resides,
Cosmic stories within the night’s tides.
Each twinkling star holds a promise bright,
Of endless wonders in the soft moonlight.

Among the petals, we find our peace,
In the silence woven, our hearts release.
Frost-kissed moments, fleeting but true,
Under starlit skies, we start anew.

Frozen Echoes of a Shining Past

In the icy breath of forgotten days,
Echoes linger in whimsical ways.
Whispers of laughter, soft and sweet,
Frozen memories where time does meet.

Snowflakes falling, each one unique,
Carry the stories that we long seek.
Golden moments wrapped in white,
Shine through the darkness, lighting the night.

The past holds treasures, glimmers of grace,
In every frost, a familiar face.
Echoing laughter dances in the air,
As we wander through dreams laid bare.

In the stillness, we pause to remember,
The warmth of summers, the glow of September.
Each frozen sigh carries a trace,
Of lives once lived, in this sacred space.

With every breath, the cold sparks delight,
Reminders of joy in the silent night.
Frozen echoes, a bridge to the past,
In winter's embrace, our memories last.

Frosted Fantasies of the Twilight Hour

In twilight's gentle sway, we dream,
Whispers of ice and silver gleam.
The world adorned in a frosted hue,
Each breath a whisper, soft and true.

Echoes linger in the crisp, still air,
Painting the night with delicate care.
Stars twinkle bright, a silent choir,
Underneath the moon's soft sapphire.

Snowflakes dance in the fading light,
Waltzing slowly into the night.
Each crystal unique, a fleeting sigh,
As shadows stretch and gently lie.

Beneath the branches, cold and bare,
Magic lingers in the night air.
Our fantasies wrapped in winter's embrace,
Soft dreams linger in this tranquil space.

Time stands still as we wander free,
In frost-kissed realms, just you and me.
The twilight hour, a sacred place,
Where all our worries vanish without trace.

Shining Traces on the White Expanse

Footsteps crunch on the gleaming snow,
As winter's beauty continues to grow.
Across the vast and silent land,
Nature whispers, hand in hand.

The sun glimmers on the frosty field,
Golden light in silver shield.
Every flake, a playful spark,
Illuminating the winter dark.

Trees stand tall, cloaked in white,
Guardians of the chilly night.
Their branches bow with heavy grace,
Each one holding a secret space.

In quiet hours, magic reigns,
Nature's art in glistening chains.
We trace our paths, our laughter bright,
On this pristine canvas of pure delight.

As day fades into twilight's embrace,
We cherish each memory, every trace.
The white expanse, a timeless tale,
In winter's embrace, we softly sail.

Fragments of a Chilly Reverie

In the hush of the early dawn,
Winter’s charm begins to yawn.
A chill wraps round like a lover’s hand,
Cradling dreams across the land.

Whispers of frost on window panes,
Echoing softly like gentle refrains.
Each breath a cloud in the morning light,
A dance of magic, pure and bright.

Moments fleeting, like snowflakes fall,
Each one a whisper, a silent call.
In dreams we weave, in soft embrace,
Fragments of time in this sacred space.

A world anew, painted in white,
Where shadows play under the soft moonlight.
The chill ignites a spark within,
A dreamy journey where we begin.

When twilight beckons, we'll find our way,
Through frosted meadows, at the end of the day.
In fragments of dreams, our hearts stay free,
We wander together in sweet reverie.

Glistening Crust Beneath the Stars

Beneath the stars, a glistening crust,
A blanket of snow, in winter we trust.
Each step we take crunches in delight,
As shadows dance in the pale moonlight.

The night sky sings with a million lights,
A symphony bright that ignites the nights.
Each star, a dream, a distant hope,
Guiding our souls as we learn to cope.

The air is crisp, sharp as a knife,
In this frozen realm, we find our life.
With hearts aglow, we cherish the chill,
For in this moment, time stands still.

Whispers of winter caress our skin,
As we share stories, breathe them in.
In glistening beauty, we find our way,
Under the stars that guide our play.

So let us wander through this night,
With laughter ringing, our spirits bright.
For beneath the crust, the world holds fast,
In winter's embrace, our hearts are cast.

A Ballet of Glimmering Diamonds

In twilight's soft embrace, they dance,
With elegance that holds a glance.
Each shimmer tells a tale untold,
A treasure of the night so bold.

They twirl and spin in dazzling light,
Their whispers echo through the night.
A ballet perfect, pure, and bright,
As diamonds glisten in moon's sight.

With every leap, a timeless grace,
They paint the sky, a stellar space.
Colors burst like dreams set free,
A festival of memory.

Through fleeting moments, beauty glows,
A symphony of light that flows.
In shadows deep, they softly play,
A dance that bids the night to stay.

As dawn approaches, dreams will cease,
But in their wake, the heart finds peace.
A ballet etched in starlit dreams,
Forever held in moonlit beams.

Iced Portraits Beneath the Stars

In stillness wrapped, the night unfolds,
With icy portraits, secrets hold.
Each crystal face, a fleeting glance,
A memory caught in silent dance.

Stars twinkle close in velvet skies,
Reflecting dreams in frozen sighs.
They whisper tales from far away,
Guiding spirits where shadows play.

The night air shimmers, crisp and bright,
As constellations paint the night.
Iced breaths emerge with chilling grace,
Each exhale, a moment to embrace.

Fragile beauty in the dark,
Illuminated by a spark.
From twilight's hold, the world stands still,
In icy frames, we feel the thrill.

With every star, a wish ignites,
In frozen echoes, heartbeats light.
These portraits tell of dreams long past,
And in their gaze, forever cast.

Chilling Beauty

Frozen whispers caress the air,
Chilling beauty, everywhere.
In dewdrops held on winter's breath,
We find the art of life's sweet death.

Icicles glisten in pale moonlight,
A landscape draped in silvery white.
The world slows down, a tender pause,
As nature draws her frozen claws.

Frost-kissed petals gently sigh,
In quiet corners where shadows lie.
Each crystal shard a silent song,
To which our weary hearts belong.

From chilly dawn to dusk's embrace,
Time loses touch with its fierce pace.
In chilling beauty, we remain,
Wrapped in whispers, free from pain.

As winter's grasp begins to fade,
We cherish all the cold parade.
For in the frost, we find the light,
A beauty born from darkest night.

Silent in Time

Moments hang in air so still,
A quiet echo, a gentle thrill.
Time suspends, a fleeting breath,
A silence wrapped in love and death.

In shadows deep, the secrets weave,
Whispers of all that we believe.
Each heartbeat echoes, soft and true,
In memories shared by me and you.

A glance exchanged, a tender sigh,
In timeless dance, we both comply.
The world outside fades into night,
As we hold on to pure delight.

Amidst the stars, we find our space,
In frozen moments, hearts embrace.
Silent in time, our spirits gleam,
Together wrapped in a waking dream.

When morning light begins to break,
And shadows whisper, hearts awake,
We'll cherish moments, soft and bright,
In silence held, our love takes flight.

Luminescent Icefields in Dreaming Night

Across the vale, a glimmer spreads,
With luminescent ice, where magic treads.
A canvas painted with frozen hues,
In dreaming nights where starlight brews.

The moon's embrace, a silver spell,
In fields of ice where spirits dwell.
Each flake, a note of whispered grace,
A symphony of light we chase.

The night unfolds its shimmering shroud,
As nature sings both soft and loud.
Through twinkling frost, the world ignites,
In luminous blooms on endless nights.

We dance along the crystal streams,
In icy swirls of fragile dreams.
Each breath exhales a sparkling song,
As we move freely, where we belong.

Through every step, the magic grows,
In fields of light, the heart just knows.
Luminescent, pure, forever bright,
Embraced beneath the dreaming night.

Faint Glows in the Depths of Frost

In the cold, whispers dance, small and bright,
Faint glimmers twinkle, hidden from sight.
Beneath the ice, shadows softly sleep,
Where secrets linger, buried deep.

Glistening paths where silence prevail,
Footsteps muffled, like a forgotten tale.
In the stillness, breath held with care,
Frigid beauty, biting the air.

Colors muted in this frosty art,
Each breath stirring a wintry heart.
Nature's canvas painted in white,
A gentle pause, a breath of light.

Through the chill, the night slowly glows,
Faint beacons rise as the cold wind blows.
A dance of stars, flickers above,
In this serene, untouched love.

Embers of warmth in the frost's cruel hand,
Igniting dreams in a frozen land.
Here in the depths, where the stillness grows,
Faint glows emerge, a silent prose.

The Enchantment of Shimmering Silence

In the hush of night, magic does weave,
Shimmering silence, we softly conceive.
Stars whisper tales in the darkened sky,
Enchanting hearts, like a gentle sigh.

Moonlight dances, casting silver gleams,
A serene glow, as soft as dreams.
Wrapped in quiet, each shadow plays,
In the enchanting night, the spirit sways.

Frozen breath hangs in the muted air,
We find solace, like a whispered prayer.
Stars may shimmer, yet silence reigns,
In the heart's echo, love remains.

A moment captured, still and clear,
In this realm where time disappears.
The enchantment thrives, a tranquil spell,
In shimmering silence, all is well.

As night deepens, the world stands still,
In this embrace, our souls can fill.
With every heartbeat, we chase the divine,
In the silence woven, your hand in mine.

A Symphony of Cold and Clarity

Frosted whispers call in the morning light,
A symphony wakes, crisp and bright.
Each crystal note, a delicate sound,
In the cold's embrace, clarity is found.

Winds weave through branches, a soft refrain,
Nature's voice whispers, free of pain.
Each breath we take, sharp and clear,
Cold stirs the heart, drawing us near.

Perfection rests in the silent flake,
A symphony born from the stillness we make.
Notes of frost blend with echoes of cheer,
In this chilly haven, nothing to fear.

The air, electric, sparks in the cold,
A vibrant chorus that never grows old.
Harmony lingers, pure and light,
In the chill of day, everything feels right.

As winter unfolds, we dance through the freeze,
In clarity's arms, we find our ease.
A play of ice, a song we adore,
In the symphony of cold, we long for more.

Tinsel Threads in the Frosty Air

Tinsel threads sparkle, caught in the breeze,
Glistening softly among the trees.
Frosty whispers weave through the night,
Embracing the world in a shimmering light.

Each strand of silver, a magic embrace,
Dancing with joy in this frosty place.
Laughter echoes in the moon's soft glow,
As tinsel threads twine, hearts all aglow.

Stars twinkle down like whispers of joy,
Filling the air like a child's pure toy.
In the stillness, magic's woven lace,
Frosty air dances, a warm embrace.

With every breath, the world turns bright,
In the heart of winter, we feel the light.
Tinsel threads shimmer, weaving a steal,
A reminder of love that we truly feel.

As dawn approaches, the vibrant dance slows,
Yet in our hearts, the enchantment grows.
Tinsel threads linger in the frosty air,
A melody found, a moment so rare.

Splinters of Light on a Chilling Surface

Frosty shards dance in the dawn,
Glistening whispers of the morn.
Each glimmer holds a tale untold,
Reflections shimmer, bright and bold.

Sunrise kisses the icy ground,
Nature's beauty, softly found.
In stillness, shadows gracefully play,
As splinters of light lead the way.

Chilled breaths form clouds in the air,
A moment paused, silent and rare.
Within this calm, there's warmth ignites,
Heartbeats dance with splinters of light.

Gentle breezes caress my skin,
Embracing all, where life begins.
Each twinkle bursts in frosty flight,
Bringing forth splinters of light.

Nature whispers in hues so bright,
Blinding visions with pure delight.
In the quiet, a promise to keep,
Through splinters of light, dreams softly seep.

Echoes of Radiance Through the Frost

In winter's hush, the echoes ring,
Radiant notes of grace they bring.
Beneath the frost, a heartbeat grows,
Whispers of warmth in winter's throes.

Through icy veins, the sunlight flows,
Dancing lightly where the cold wind blows.
Each echo sung, a story spun,
A melody felt, never done.

Crystals glisten, like stars at night,
Capture the chance to shimmer bright.
In the stillness, they call, they plead,
Echoes of love in nature's creed.

Amidst the frost, soft voices rise,
Cascading waves that mesmerize.
Hear the whispers in the air,
As radiance spreads, everywhere.

In these moments, the heart takes flight,
Within the echoes, pure delight.
Through the frost, it finds its course,
Awakening life, with radiant force.

Asphalt Canvas of a Cold Pastel

Strokes of grey on a muted street,
Life unfolds beneath hurried feet.
Whispers echo, tales of old,
On asphalt canvases, secrets told.

Pastel skies bleed into the night,
Fading colors blend, lose their fight.
In the chill, memories drift away,
As shadows linger where dreams lay.

Footsteps echo, a rhythm defined,
Marking a journey through unconfined.
Cold air breathes life into each scene,
As we wander, in between.

The pavement tells of a world long lost,
Of laughter, joy, and bitter frost.
In every crack, a memory stays,
Brushed upon the asphalt's grays.

Like a canvas, it holds our past,
In fleeting moments, we are cast.
With each step forward, a story spun,
On cold roads where our lives begun.

The Icy Symphony of a Night’s Silence

In twilight's grip, the silence hums,
An icy symphony softly comes.
Notes of stillness float through the air,
Wrapped in shadows, everywhere.

Stars blink softly, their glow so bright,
Playing chords in the deep of night.
The moon weaves tales in silver lace,
Guiding dreams through this hidden space.

Whispers of wind in the world confined,
Weaving moments, perfectly aligned.
Chilled serenades dance on the breeze,
As night unfolds with effortless ease.

In the quiet, hearts resonate,
Each beat a note, we celebrate.
The frosty air holds secrets tight,
In the icy symphony of night.

Every breath, a perfect refrain,
An orchestra formed from joy and pain.
Within the calm, a magic lies,
In the silence, a world that flies.

Prismatic Mist in a Frigid Embrace

In the still of night, mist holds tight,
Colors dance beneath the moon's light.
Whispers echo, secrets unfold,
A canvas of dreams in the cold.

Shadows linger where the frost bites,
Veils of wonder in the pale lights.
Each breath a cloud in the chilling air,
Nature's painting, vivid and rare.

Crisp whispers of wind through the trees,
Awakening life with gentle ease.
The world is cloaked in a shimmering haze,
As time fades softly, lost in a daze.

Glimmers reflect on the icy stream,
Reality bends like a fleeting dream.
Footsteps muffled on powdery ground,
In this embrace, solace is found.

The prism of colors begins to fade,
As dawn approaches, night's parade.
Yet the memory clings to the day,
In every heart where dreams hang and sway.

Celestial Shimmers of Frosted Time

Stars twinkle like diamonds in the sky,
Each one a secret, each glow a sigh.
Frost paints the world with delicate grace,
Time whispers softly in this tranquil space.

The moon hangs low, a silent queen,
Casting light on the blankets of green.
Crystals of ice catch the soft glow,
Creating a landscape where wonders flow.

Moments freeze in the frigid air,
Captured forever, they linger there.
Echoes of laughter dance on the breeze,
A tapestry woven with effortless ease.

In the stillness, memories collide,
Reflecting the shadows where dreams abide.
The world glows softly in twilight's embrace,
Each shimmer a trace of a time and place.

Celestial beauty, a frosted rhyme,
Holds us captive, suspended in time.
While the universe sings, we stand in wonder,
In this frosty realm, we dream and ponder.

Veils of Chill Draped Over Twilight

Twilight descends, cloaked in a shroud,
Veils of chill gather, silent and proud.
The sun dips low, bidding goodbye,
As shadows stretch and softly sigh.

Frozen whispers through the barren trees,
Embrace the night, carried by the breeze.
The world takes a breath, wrapped in still,
Nature rests quietly, her dreams to fulfill.

Stars emerge like jewels in the night,
Piercing the veil with a twinkling light.
Each one a story, each glow a call,
Inviting us closer, enchanting us all.

The landscape transforms in the dimming glow,
A canvas of wonders, shimmering slow.
Frost-kissed leaves weave tales of the day,
As night softly cradles the world in its sway.

Veils of chill whisper secrets untold,
In the heart of the night, the magic unfolds.
With each passing moment, enchantment draws near,
In twilight's embrace, all is crystal clear.

Crystals of Reflection on Winter's Edge

Morning breaks on winter's edge,
Crystals glimmer in a perfect hedge.
The world awakens, draped in white,
A frosted wonder, a pure delight.

Gnarly branches with diamonds adorned,
Sparkle and shine as the day is born.
Each droplet a mirror, each ray a thread,
Weaving a tapestry where dreams are fed.

Softly the snowflakes begin their dance,
Falling like wishes, the heart's romance.
The landscape muffled, wrapped tight in love,
A whisper of magic sent from above.

On the edge of winter where stillness reigns,
Crystals reflect all our joys and pains.
Footprints linger in the soft snow,
Stories untold in the quiet below.

As dusk appears with a silken hue,
The world changes form, all feels anew.
Crystals of reflection cradle our dreams,
On winter's edge, life softly gleams.

Twilight's Touch on Glacial Layers

As daylight fades, the ice does glow,
Soft hues of pink and amber flow.
The tranquil stillness wraps the land,
A frozen canvas, nature's hand.

Glistening shards catch the last light,
Whispers of beauty in falling night.
Each crevice holds a secret bright,
In twilight's touch, all feels just right.

Crystals dance beneath the stars,
Illuminated like distant mars.
Awakening dreams in the winter air,
A symphony of silence, beyond compare.

Time slows down as the cold descends,
Nature whispers; the magic bends.
Guiding hearts through chill and grace,
In twilight's embrace, we find our place.

Forever etched in icy blue,
Moments captured, fleeting, true.
As shadows stretch, the day takes flight,
In glacial layers, we find our light.

A Glint of Hope in the Winter's Calm

In the hush of winter's breath,
A glint of hope stirs life from death.
With every flake that graces the ground,
A promise of warmth begins to sound.

Beneath the frost, the earth does dream,
Of budding blooms in the sun's warm beam.
In silent woods where shadows play,
Dawn's soft glow keeps despair at bay.

Icicles hang like crystal tears,
Reflecting light that calms our fears.
Each fragile moment, a fleeting spark,
In winter's calm, we find our mark.

Branches heavy with snow's caress,
Nature whispers in soft tenderness.
A world transformed, so pure and white,
In the stillness, we weave our flight.

As seasons change and time moves on,
Hope glimmers faint, like a delicate dawn.
In each heartbeat, a silent song,
Winter's calm teaches us to be strong.

Glimmering Shards from Nature's Cradle

From nature's cradle, gems unfold,
Glimmering shards, a sight to behold.
In every corner, beauty breathes,
Among the branches, under the leaves.

Wander the path where sunlight spills,
Past silver streams and the rolling hills.
Nature's canvas painted bright,
A world of wonder, pure delight.

Glimmers dance on the morning dew,
A secret language, known by a few.
The forest hums a sacred tune,
In harmony with the rising moon.

Each petal glows in the softest breeze,
Symphonies played among the trees.
Whispers of life echo and soar,
In nature's arms, we're forevermore.

A treasure chest, endless in sights,
Glimmering shards beneath the lights.
Reconnect with the earth, so fair,
In nature's cradle, love is rare.

Whispers of Radiance in a Frozen Realm

In a frozen realm where silence sings,
Whispers of radiance take their wings.
In icy breath, the wonders gleam,
Each frozen moment, a fleeting dream.

Amidst the frost where shadows blend,
Nature's magic has grace to lend.
A tapestry woven with threads of light,
Glowing softly through the night.

Mountains stand like sentinels tall,
Guarding secrets they cannot call.
In crystal silence, hearts awaken,
The frozen beauty, never shaken.

Stars twinkle down with gentle grace,
Illuminating every space.
The world aglow, just out of reach,
In whispers of radiance, it seeks to teach.

So tread lightly on this sacred ground,
In every silence, a truth is found.
In the frozen still, let your spirit roam,
Whispers of warmth, leading us home.

Ghostly Glimmers on the Edge of Night

Whispers drift through shadowed trees,
Softly glowing, like a tease.
In the dark, they dance and sway,
Elusive spirits, lost in play.

Moonlight spills on glistening leaves,
Casting spells that time deceives.
Flicker faint, then fade away,
In the twilight's calm ballet.

Echoes of the past now call,
Through the night’s enchanting thrall.
Each glimmer tells a tale of yore,
In the silence, they explore.

Shadows weave between the light,
Haunting dreams in endless night.
A dance of phantoms, soft and bright,
Ghostly glimmers, pure delight.

As dawn approaches, they retreat,
Leaving only whispers sweet.
In our hearts, they linger still,
Ghostly glimmers, time to fill.

Celestial Jewels on the Frozen Field

Stars embrace the winter ground,
In the silence, beauty found.
Glistening on the snow's white bed,
Celestial jewels, softly spread.

Twinkling bright, they light the way,
Guiding dreams till break of day.
Each frost-kissed gem, a tale to tell,
In the hush, they cast a spell.

Underneath the vast, dark dome,
They remind us we're not alone.
Cosmic wonders, taking flight,
Celestial jewels in winter's night.

Silent whispers fill the air,
As the cold winds gently dare.
Breath of starlight in each breeze,
An embrace that aims to please.

In the frost, our hopes alight,
Held in dreams of shimmering light.
Celestial jewels, forever bright,
On this frozen field, take flight.

The Lattice of Winter’s Embrace

Fractals woven, crisp and bright,
Nature’s art in purest light.
Branches lace the frosty air,
A lattice formed with tender care.

Every flake a story spun,
Underneath the pale sun.
Whispers dance in chilly breeze,
Winter's embrace, soft as these.

Patterns shift with every sigh,
As the winter clouds drift by.
In the stillness, beauty grows,
The lattice blooms where cold winds blow.

Twilight deepens, shadows blend,
In the web, the night descends.
Each crystal glimmers, pure and bright,
In the tapestry of night.

Breath of winter, crisp and clear,
Echoes fade, yet draw us near.
In this fold of time and space,
We find warmth in winter's grace.

Prismatic Dreams in the Snow

Colors swirl in winter's hush,
Painting dreams with every brush.
Violet, blue, and fiery red,
In the snow, they dance ahead.

Fractured light on white expanse,
Each reflection, a fleeting glance.
Nature's canvas, bright and bold,
Prismatic visions, tales unfold.

In the chill, the colors play,
Guiding lost souls on their way.
Whispers echo through the night,
Dreams adorned with purest light.

A shiver runs through frozen ground,
In this realm, new hopes abound.
Fleeting moments, vivid sights,
Prismatic dreams in starry nights.

As the dawn approaches near,
Colors fade but do not disappear.
In our hearts, these dreams reside,
Prismatic visions, our winter guide.

Whispered Secrets of the Icebound Horizon

Beneath the sky, a secret waits,
Silent whispers of winter's fates.
Snowflakes dance on a frozen breeze,
Echoes of nature, calm and freeze.

Crystals form like gentle sighs,
In the stillness, the heart complies.
A world wrapped in frost, so divine,
Time unwinds in a silver line.

Mountains loom, their spirits strong,
Guardians of winter's ancient song.
Each breath exhaled, a fragile art,
Painting warmth in a cold heart.

Glistening trails on icy paths,
Footsteps follow through winter's wrath.
Eyes behold the shimmering view,
A canvas bright, a world anew.

Secrets whispered in the chill,
Nature's quiet, a soothing thrill.
Among the pines, truth softly lies,
In the depths where silence ties.

Chilled Euphoria in Silvery Hues

Beneath a veil of soft white glow,
Where laughter dances, pure and slow.
The chill wraps round like a warm embrace,
In every flake, a fleeting grace.

Whispers of joy in the frosty air,
Moments treasured, beyond compare.
Each breath a cloud, a dream in flight,
Chilled euphoria, heart's delight.

Trees adorned in silver lace,
Nature's wonder, a wondrous space.
Glimmers sparkle in soft sunlight,
Inviting souls to bask in light.

Wrapped in layers, soft and warm,
We find a way to weather the storm.
With every step, a new design,
A world alive, where hearts align.

In the hush, all worries fade,
A sanctuary that we have made.
Where friendships blossom, spirits soar,
Chilled euphoria, forevermore.

A Tapestry Woven from Ice and Light

In the dawn's glow, a tapestry gleams,
Woven from whispers and frozen dreams.
Threads of silver, spun with care,
A mosaic bright, beyond compare.

Snowflakes weave into patterns rare,
Nature's artistry, its breath laid bare.
With each heartbeat, the colors flow,
A story told in the frost and glow.

Hues of azure, hints of gold,
Crafting secrets, waiting to be told.
The shimmering fabric of winter's night,
A canvas alive, pure and bright.

Every shadow, a tale to relay,
In this realm where the warm hearts stay.
Light dances gently on icy skin,
Healing whispers from deep within.

Together we stand, in awe of the sight,
A world reborn through ice and light.
Embracing the chill, we dare to dream,
In this beautiful tapestry, we gleam.

Frosty Cascade in the Heart of Winter

In the heart of winter, a cascade flows,
Where frosty whispers tell of the snows.
Rushing waters, cloaked in ice,
Nature's wonder, a sacrifice.

Glimmers sparkle, a diamond stream,
Carving paths in the frozen dream.
Each ripple sings a melody,
Of a world spun from tranquility.

Frozen branches bow with grace,
As the winter breeze finds its place.
A frosty dance, a swirling sight,
In the chilly embrace of the night.

The cascade flows, both wild and free,
Filling hearts with sweet reverie.
In every splash, a spark of cheer,
A frosty cascade, forever near.

Through the silence, time may bend,
In winter's arms, we find a friend.
A moment held, as snowflakes twirl,
In this frosty lie, our dreams unfurl.

Milton Keynes UK
Ingram Content Group UK Ltd.
UKHW010230111224
452348UK00011B/638

9 789916 798775